GOLDEN STATE

THE BRAZILLER SERIES OF POETRY
Richard Howard, General Editor

GOLDEN STATE

by

FRANK BIDART

with a note by Richard Howard

GEORGE BRAZILLER

New York

Published simultaneously in Canada by Doubleday, Canada, Ltd.
All rights reserved.
For information, address the publisher:
George Braziller, Inc.
One Park Avenue, New York 10016

Standard Book Number: 0–8076–0676–6, cloth
0–8076–0677–4, paper
Library of Congress Card Number: 72–94953
First Printing
Printed in the United States of America
Designed by Harry Ford and Kathleen Carey

Contents

FRANK BIDART

"Hell came when I saw MYSELF . . ."

Not familiarity but recognition is the craving here, a thirst not for knowledge but acknowledgment, not likeness but identity. And it must be put this way—in the way of choices entertained and rejected, hesitations, bewilderments, refusals. It would be out of the question to speak (as we are so fond of speaking) of "unerring aims," of "sure instincts," when their object is precisely errant, indeterminate: when the target is the realization of life itself, and the errors the very means whereby any aim—focus, concentration, scope—may be achieved.

A young man, a young poet, cannot discover the true goals of his endeavor without discarding the false ones. The wrong turns, the missing links and mistaken signals are no more than evidence of what may be right, given, understood. Over this book is suspended, like a ceiling of swords, the threat and indeed the doom of the negative. In his prosody, as in his convulsive pursuit of a voice which will, accountably, speak in the first person singular —and of course the achieved value here is that the prosody is not apart from but is a part of the pursuit, it *is* the pursuit at its incandescent brimstone pitch—Frank Bidart is as evasive as he is venturesome. "Don't turn into the lies/of mere, neat poetry . . ." he implores his father *in his own poetry*, and he will be at pains to keep the utterance from being *mere*, from becoming *neat*. Everywhere is the effort to vary the cadence, to elude that kind of recuperation of energy, that avowal of a constant in verbal behavior which (precisely because it can be repeated, violated, returned to) we call *verse*. This is a poetry which is, as Heidegger calls it in his 1950 essay "Language," *purely spoken;* its roots are not in assent, which is silent, but in declaration, in contestation, which is the lesson of all speech. "The opposite of what is purely spoken, the opposite of the poem," Heidegger says, "is not prose. Pure prose is never 'prosaic'. It is as poetic and hence as rare as poetry." Prose, then, is the basis of Frank Bidart's prosody, his organization of language to suit and serve his need, which is his quest: a poetry in search of itself. Such a petition will necessarily invoke a warp of the formal enterprises—the novel and the play, ever since Proust and Pirandello made the Search explicit thematically, which is to say formally, afford the clue here, the way into the labyrinth. The way out, however, is one that Bidart has had to find by himself: if poetry is prose, then the poem must have that form of its own which is *not* a novel, *not* a play. And he has found that form (cunningly enjambed, weighted with the varying shifts of the raised voice, the wounded utterance) in the *terrain vague* between the dream and the letter, the only two forms of human expression which are not subject to revision, but merely to creation. Bidart's *dream letters*, then, are that form, as astounding in their mythologizing remove as in their intimacy, their avowals.

Undressing, Oscar Wilde once told someone, is romance, dressing philanthropy; and the poet who is neither romantic nor philanthropic, merely questing his own creation as a poet, is indeed endangered, likely to be severed from himself by the one sword or the other. It is interesting to see how Bidart avoids the cutting edges: he begins and ends his book with "other lives," mirror-images of what, in his center section, he explores indeed as the *given*. Shocking as "Herbert White" is intended to be—and shocking it is—there is every reason for it to precede the rest, for this poem's real horror is its parallel with the discovery made in the closing poem "Another Life," the *identical* discovery that the self must become one with its unacknowledged obsession, that there is only the one life, not other lives. Dressing, then, is how the book begins, for it is Bidart's tactical decision to open with an "autobiographical" narrative which is not his own, thereby preparing us to accept his ulterior revelations, his undressing as fictions, as mythologized identities, not confessions:

... The way to approach freedom
was to acknowledge necessity:—
I sensed I had to become not merely
a speaker, the "eye," but a character ...

The ambitions of a self which can engorge Catullus and Aeneas
—versions of the poet and the hero which would seem, everywhere else in this troubling, attractive book, to be cut off from
expressive means: what a thing it is to have an education!—are
immense indeed, and they are ransomed (if ambitions can be
ransomed, rather than merely reduced or rewarded) by the earn-
ings of *presence*, which we sometimes call wit:

> ... leave me *alone*!

He smirked, and said
I was never alone.

> I told him to go to hell.

He said that this was hell.

Which way I fly is hell, myself am hell is the ultimate Satanic
assertion, and one which Bidart has made, wittily and sometimes
with a wonderful lyric warp to his prose ("I turned, and turned,
but now all that was left/was an enormous/fresco;—on each side,
the unreadable/fresco of my life ..."), into a thesaurus of detesta-
tions, heresies, the scandal—for poetry—of the negative. A clear
case, then, or a clarified one, of diabolic possession; the recording
angel of Bidart's world is a fallen one: himself. "What *reaches*
him," he asks in the poem "Self-Portrait," "except disaster?" By
the end of the book we know—it is no longer what reaches him
but what *he* can reach, the colonization of inferno. And hell lay
all before him, where to choose. ...

RICHARD HOWARD

Part One

HERBERT WHITE

"When I hit her on the head, it was good,

and then I did it to her a couple of times,—
but it was funny,—afterwards,
it was as if somebody else did it . . .

Everything flat, without sharpness, richness or line.

Still, I liked to drive past the woods where she lay,
tell the old lady and the kids I had to take a piss,
hop out and do it to her . . .

The whole buggy of them waiting for me
                                        made me feel good;
but still, just like I knew all along,
                            she didn't move.

When the body got too discomposed,
I'd just jack off, letting it fall on her . . .

—It sounds crazy, but I tell you
sometimes it was *beautiful*—; I don't know how
to say it, but for a minute, *everything* was possible—;
and then,
then,—
        well, like I said, she didn't move: and I saw,
under me, a little girl was just lying there in the mud:

and I knew I couldn't have done that,—
somebody *else* had to have done that,—

standing above her there,
                        in those ordinary, shitty leaves . . .

—One time, I went to see Dad in a motel where he was
staying with a woman; but she was gone;
you could smell the wine in the air; and he started,
real embarrassing, to cry . . .
                              He was still a little drunk,
and asked me to forgive him for
all he hadn't done—; but, What the shit?
Who would have wanted to stay with Mom? with bastards
not even his own kids?

                    I got in the truck, and started to drive,
and saw a little girl—
who I picked up, hit on the head, and
screwed, and screwed, and screwed, and screwed, then

buried,
        in the garden of the motel . . .

—You see, ever since I was a kid I wanted
to *feel* things make sense: I remember

looking out the window of my room back home,—
and being almost suffocated by the asphalt;
and grass; and trees; and glass;
just *there*, just *there*, doing nothing!
not saying anything! filling me up—
but also being a wall; dead, and stopping me;
—how I wanted to see beneath it, cut

beneath it, and make it
somehow, come alive . . .

                    The salt of the earth;
Mom once said, 'Man's spunk is the salt of the earth . . .'

—That night, at that Twenty-nine Palms Motel
I had passed a million times on the road, everything

fit together; was alright;
it seemed like
                everything *had* to be there, like I had spent years
trying, and at last finally finished drawing this
                                huge circle . . .

—But then, suddenly I knew
somebody *else* did it, some bastard
had hurt a little girl—; the motel
                        I could see again, it had been
itself all the time, a lousy
pile of bricks, plaster, that didn't seem to
have to be there,—but *was*, just by chance . . .

—Once, on the farm, when I was a kid,
I was screwing a goat; and the rope around his neck
when he tried to get away
pulled tight;—and just when I came,
he *died* . . .
                I came back the next day; jacked off over his body;
but it didn't do any good . . .

Mom once said:
'Man's spunk is the salt of the earth, and grows kids.'

I tried so hard to come; more *pain* than anything else;
but didn't do any good . . .

—About six months ago, I heard Dad remarried,
so I drove over to Connecticut to see him and see

if he was happy.
       She was twenty-five years younger than him:
she had lots of little kids, and I don't know why,
I felt shaky . . .

       I stopped in front of the address; and
snuck up to the window to look in . . .
                    —There he was, a kid
six months old on his lap, laughing
and bouncing the kid, happy in his old age
to play the papa after years of sleeping around,—
it twisted me up . . .
              To think that what he wouldn't give me,
              he *wanted* to give them . . .

       I could have killed the bastard . . .

—Naturally, I just got right back in the car,
and believe me, was determined, determined,
to head straight for home . . .

                    but the more I drove,
I kept thinking about getting a girl,
and the more I thought I shouldn't do it,
the more I had to—

              I saw her coming out of the movies,
saw she was alone, and
kept circling the blocks as she walked along them,
saying, 'You're going to leave her alone.'
'You're going to leave her alone.'

              —The woods were scary!
As the seasons changed, and you saw more and more

of the skull show through, the nights became clearer,
and the buds,—erect, like nipples . . .

—But then, one night,
nothing *worked* . . .
                      Nothing in the sky
would blur like I wanted it to;
and I couldn't, *couldn't,*

get it to seem to me
that somebody *else* did it . . .

I tried, and tried, but there was just me there,
and her, and the sharp trees
saying, 'That's you standing there.
                  You're . . .
                        just you.'

          I hope I fry.

—Hell came when I saw
            MYSELF . . .
                  and couldn't stand

what I see . . ."

He's *still* young—; thirty, but looks younger—
or does he? . . . In the eyes and cheeks, tonight,
turning in the mirror, he saw his mother,—
puffy; angry; bewildered . . . Many nights
now, when he stares there, he gets angry:—
something *unfulfilled* there, something dead
to what he once thought he surely could be—
Now, just the glamour of habits . . .

                                    Once, instead,
he thought insight would remake him, he'd reach
—what? The thrill, the exhilaration
unravelling disaster, that seemed to teach
necessary knowledge . . . became just jargon.

Sick of being decent, he craves another
crash. What *reaches* him except disaster?

Part Two

CALIFORNIA PLUSH

The only thing I miss about Los Angeles

is the Hollywood Freeway at midnight, windows down and
radio blaring
bearing right into the center of the city, the Capitol Tower
on the right, and beyond it, Hollywood Boulevard
blazing

—pimps, surplus stores, footprints of the stars

—descending through the city
                fast as the law would allow

through the lights, then rising to the stack
out of the city
to the stack where lanes are stacked six deep

            and you on top; the air
            now clean; for a moment weightless

                  without memories, or
                  need for a past.

The need for the past

is so much at the center of my life
I write this poem to record my discovery of it,
my reconciliation.

It was in Bishop, the room was done
in California plush: we had gone into the coffee shop, were told
you could only get a steak in the bar:
                              I hesitated,
not wanting to be an occasion of temptation for my father

but he wanted to, so we entered

a dark room, with amber water glasses, walnut
tables, captain's chairs,
plastic doilies, papier-mâché bas-relief wall ballerinas,
German memorial plates "bought on a trip to Europe,"
Puritan crosshatch green-yellow wallpaper,
frilly shades, cowhide
booths—

I thought of Cambridge:

              the lovely congruent elegance
              of Revolutionary architecture, even of

ersatz thirties Georgian

seemed alien, a threat, sign
of all I was not—

to bode order and lucidity

as an ideal, if not reality—

not this California plush, which

              also

I was not.

And so I made myself an Easterner,
finding it, after all, more like me
than I had let myself hope.

And now, staring into the embittered face of
my father,

again, for two weeks, as twice a year,
I was back.

The waitress asked us if we wanted a drink.
Grimly, I waited until he said no . . .

Before the tribunal of the world I submit the following
document:

Nancy showed it to us,
in her apartment in the motel,
as she waited month by month
for the property settlement, her children grown
and working for their father,
at fifty-three now alone,
a drink in her hand:

as my father said,
"They keep a drink in her hand":

Name   Wallace Du Bois
Box No   128   *Chino, Calif.*
Date   July 25   *,19*   54

Mr Howard Arturian
I am writing a letter to you this afternoon while
I'm in the mood of writing. How is everything getting along

with you these fine days, as for me everything is just fine and
I feel great except for the heat I think its lot warmer then it
is up there but I don't mind it so much. I work at the dairy
half day and I go to trade school the other half day Body &
Fender, now I am learning how to spray paint cars I've already
painted one and now I got another car to paint. So now I
think I've learned all I want after I have learned all this. I
know how to straighten metals and all that. I forgot to say
"Hello" to you. The reason why I am writing to you is about
a job, my Parole Officer told me that he got letter from and
that you want me to go to work for you. So I wanteded to
know if its truth. When I go to the Board in Feb. I'll tell them
what I want to do and where I would like to go, so if you
want me to work for you I'd rather have you sent me to your
brother John in Tonapah and place to stay for my family.
The Old Lady says the same thing in her last letter that she
would be some place else then in Bishop, thats the way I feel
too. and another thing is my drinking problem. I made up
my mind to quit my drinking, after all what it did to me and
what happen.

This is one thing I'll never forget as longs as I live I never
want to go through all this mess again. This sure did teach me
lot of things that I never knew before. So Howard you can
let me know soon as possible. I sure would appreciate it.

P. S   From Your Friend
I hope you can read my   Wally Du Bois
writing. I am a little nervous yet

—He and his wife had given a party, and
one of the guests was walking away
just as Wallace started backing up his car.
He hit him, so put the body in the back seat

and drove to a deserted road.
There he put it before the tires, and
ran back and forth over it several times.

When he got out of Chino, he did,
indeed, never do that again:
but one child was dead, his only son,
found with the rest of the family
immobile in their beds with typhoid,
next to the mother, the child having been
dead two days:

he continued to drink, and as if it were the Old West
shot up the town a couple of Saturday nights.

"So now I think I've learned all I want
after I have learned all this: this sure did teach me a lot of things
that I never knew before.
I am a little nervous yet."

It seems to me
an emblem of Bishop—

For watching the room, as the waitresses in their
back-combed, Parisian, peroxided, bouffant hairdos,
and plastic belts,
moved back and forth

I thought of Wallace, and
the room suddenly seemed to me
        not uninteresting at all:

        they were the same. Every plate and chair

had its congruence with

all the choices creating

these people, created

by them—by me,

for this is my father's chosen country, my origin.

Before, I had merely been anxious, bored; now,
I began to ask a thousand questions . . .

He was, of course, mistrustful, knowing I was bored,
knowing he had dragged me up here from Bakersfield

after five years

of almost managing to forget Bishop existed.

But he soon became loquacious, ordered a drink,
and settled down for
an afternoon of talk . . .

He liked Bishop: somehow, it was to his taste, this
hard-drinking, loud, visited-by-movie-stars town.
"Better to be a big fish in a little pond."

And he was: when they came to shoot a film,
he entertained them; Miss A——, who wore
nothing at all under her mink coat; Mr. M——,
good horseman, good shot.

"But when your mother
let me down" (for alcoholism and

infidelity, she divorced him)
"and Los Angeles wouldn't give us water any more,
I had to leave.

We were the first people to grow potatoes in this valley."

When he began to tell me
that he lost control of the business
because of the settlement he gave my mother,

because I had heard it
many times,

in revenge, I asked why people up here drank so much.

He hesitated. "Bored, I guess.
—Not much to do."

And why had Nancy's husband left her?

In bitterness, all he said was:
"People up here drink too damn much."

And that was how experience
had informed his life.

"So now I think I've learned all I want
after I have learned all this: this sure did teach me a lot of things
that I never knew before.
I am a little nervous yet."

Yet, as my mother said,
returning, as always, to the past,

"I wouldn't change any of it.
It taught me so much. Gladys
is such an innocent creature: you look into her face
and somehow it's empty, all she worries about
are sales and the baby.
Her husband's too good!"

It's quite pointless to call this rationalization:
my mother, for uncertain reasons, has had her
bout with insanity, but she's right:

the past in maiming us,
makes us,
fruition
     is also
destruction:

        I think of Proust, dying
in a cork-lined room, because he refuses to eat
because he thinks that he cannot write if he eats
because he wills to write, to finish his novel

—his novel which recaptures the past, and
with a kind of joy, because
in the debris
of the past, he has found the sources of the necessities

which have led him to this room, writing

—in this strange harmony, does he will
for it to have been different?

        And I can't *not* think of the remorse of Oedipus,

who tries to escape, to expiate the past
by blinding himself, and
then, when he is dying, sees that he has become a Daimon

—does he, discovering, at last, this cruel
coherence created by
                            "the order of the universe"

—does he will
anything reversed?

                        I look at my father:
as he drinks his way into garrulous, shaky
defensiveness, the debris of the past
is just debris—; whatever I reason, it is a desolation
to watch . . .

must I watch?
He will not change; he does not *want* to change;

every defeated gesture implies
the past is useless, irretrievable . . .
—I want to change: I want to stop fear's subtle

guidance of my life—; but, how can I do that
if I am still
afraid of its source?

                        1966–67

I once knew a man named Snake.

He killed
All our snakes.

One day one bit him.

"Ha-ya feelin', Snake?"
I asked when he returned.

He said,
"My name is Walter."

The brown house
on the brown hill
reminds me of my parents.

Its memory is of poverty,
not merely poverty of means,
but poverty of history, of awareness of
the ways men have found to live.

My stepfather was from Texas.

"Niggers, you know they're different from us,
they go mad when they make love,
we white men have to watch out or women

won't have anything to do with us."

(*pause*) "Back in McKinney, there's a spot on the pavement
where they caught a nigger who'd raped a white woman,

right there they tied him down,
poured gasoline on him, and
lit him afire.
—You can still see the mark."

Illuminated by the lore of the past, justified
by the calluses on his hands,
—won walking round and round
a wheel digging a water
well fourteen hours a day—
he was happy with himself.

> Before my mother married him, she was
> free for several years, proposed to
> by several men we may call,
> in this context,

> "educated"

(a lawyer; a doctor; unconfident men
sharing a certain unmistakable
humaneness)

> and later, she often asked herself

> why she married him.

She would laugh, and say, "I always liked the horse's asses!"

(*pause*) "My mother never told me about these things."

Its memory is of poverty,
not merely poverty of means,

but poverty of history, of awareness of
the ways men have found to live.

My father
"was the handsomest man in Kern County."

When they met, he was eight years older, and

driving a truck for a bootlegger.

He had had a dance studio in Hollywood,
gone broke, and

was back. "He introduced me to a fast, drinking crowd; my
        God,

we smoked—! And I wore lipstick: Olive and I promised each
        other

we would never do that."

So he went back into farming, as he had done as a child
when his father died, and
"was a genius."

"Your father, on our wedding night, told me
he had ninety-two thousand dollars in the bank. His first
potato crop. He didn't have a dime the year before."

But he
spent all the afternoons in the cool bars.
"He always was a sucker for a no-good

bum with a slick line and a good story.
How an intelligent man like that—"

Soon he
was an alcoholic, and unfaithful; unfaithful
many times; which fact was, as it were,
brought home to her, by
detectives. She would shake her head:

"How an intelligent man like that—"

(*bitterly*) "He never would have made us a real home,
the way decent men do."

In her own illness, when she began to
try to turn brass and tin into gold
by boiling them in a large pot full of
soap, cat's fur, and orange rinds,

she was following

the teachings of the Rosicrucians,

the secrets of the past, the mysteries of the

pyramids.

> Later, as she began
> to be well, she would ask,

"Why did it happen?

> It seems to
say something awful about

everything I've done.
                                    Does it make everything wrong?
I knew so little
all along!"

(*pause*) "Why did it happen to *me*—at

forty-eight?"

Its memory is of poverty,
not merely poverty of means,
but poverty of history, of awareness of
the ways men have found to live.

                            For men are not
                            children, who learn
                            not to touch the burner; men,

unlike Walter,
cannot simply revert

to their true names.
                    The brown clapboard house,
in spite of its fine pioneer tradition,
because of the absence of the knowledge in its
lines of other architecture, because of the
poverty of its

brown, barren hill,

reminds me of my parents.

                                    1966

GOLDEN STATE

I

To see my father
lying in pink velvet, a rosary
twined around his hands, rouged,
lipsticked, his skin marble . . .

My mother said, "He looks the way he did
thirty years ago, the day we got married,—
I'm *glad* I went;
I was afraid: now I can remember him
like that . . ."

Ruth, your last girlfriend, who wouldn't sleep with you
or marry, because you wanted her
to pay half the expenses, and "His drinking
almost drove me crazy—"
                              Ruth once saw you
staring into a mirror,
in your ubiquitous kerchief and cowboy hat,
say:
      "Why can't I look like a cowboy?"

You left a bag of money; and were
the unhappiest man
I have ever known well.

11

It's in many ways
a relief to have you dead.
                              I have more money.
Bakersfield is easier: life isn't so nude,
now that I no longer have to
face you each evening: mother is progressing
beautifully in therapy, I can almost convince myself
a good analyst would have saved you:

for I *need* to believe, as
always, that your pervasive sense of disappointment

proceeded from
trivial desires: but I fear
that beneath the wish to be a movie star,
cowboy, empire builder, all those
cheap desires, lay
radical disaffection
                              from the very possibilities
of human life . . .

Your wishes were too simple:
                    or too complex.

III

I find it difficult to imagine you
in bed, making love to a woman . . .

By common consensus, you were a *good* lover:
and yet,
mother once said: "Marriage would be better
if it weren't mixed up with sex . . ."

Just after the divorce,—when I was
about five,—I slept all night with you

in a motel, and again and again
you begged me
to beg her to come back . . .

I said nothing; but she went back
several times, again and again
you would go on a binge, there would be
another woman,
mother would leave . . .

You always said,
"Your mother is the only woman I've ever loved."

IV

Oh Shank, don't turn into the lies
of mere, neat poetry . . .

I've been reading Jung, and he says that we can
never get to the bottom
of what is, or was . . .

But *why* things were as they were
obsesses; I know that you
the necessity to contend with you
your *helplessness*
before yourself,
                    —has been at the center
of how I think my life . . .

                    And yet your voice, raw,
demanding, dissatisfied,
saying over the telephone:

    "How are all those bastards at Harvard?"

remains, challenging: beyond all the
patterns and paradigms
                    I use to silence and stop it.

V

I dreamed I *had* my wish:
                    —I seemed to see
the conditions of my life, upon
a luminous stage: how I could change,
how I could not: the root of necessity,
and choice.
              The stage was labelled
"Insight."
              The actors there
had no faces, I cannot remember
the patterns of their actions, but
simply by watching,

I knew that beneath my feet
the fixed stars
governing my life

had begun to fall, and melt . . .
                    —Then your face appeared,

laughing at the simplicity of my wish.

VI

Almost every day
I take out the letter you wrote me in Paris.
. . . Why?

It was written
the year before you married Shirley; Myrtle,
your girlfriend, was an ally of mine
because she "took care of you,"
but you always
made it clear
she was too dumpy and crude to marry . . .

In some ways "elegant,"
with a pencil-thin, neatly clipped moustache,
chiselled, Roman nose, you were
a millionaire
and always pretended
you couldn't afford to go to Europe . . .

When I was a child,
you didn't seem to care if I existed.

                    Bakersfield, Calif
                    July 9, 1961

Dear Pinon.
    Sorry I haven't wrote to you sooner but glad to hear that
you are well and enjoying *Paris.*

I got your fathers day wire in the hospital where I put in about twelve days but I am very well now. I quit the ciggeretts but went through ten days of hell quitting and my back had been giving me hell.

It had been very hot here but the last few days has been very nice. Emily just got out of the hospital yesterday. She had her feet worked on. I guess she will tell you about it. Glad to hear you are learning some French.

We are just about through with potatoes. Crop was very good but no price at all whitch made it a poor year. Cattle are cheap too. It look like a bad year for all farmer's.

I don't know anything else to tell you. Take care of your self and enjoy it. Maybe you will never have another chance for another trip. I don't think I'll ever get the chance to go, so if you run into a extra special gal between 28 & 35 send her over here to me as all I know over here don't amount to mutch. Well I guess I'll close now as I am going over to see Emily.

Hoping to hear from you right away.

This address is 4019 Eton St. be sure and get it straight. Myrtle would like to know how much that watch amounts to. Let us know

Will close now and write soon.

Love 'Shank'

P.S. Excuse this writing as its about 30 years since I wrote a letter.

VII

How can I say this?
                    I think my psychiatrist
likes me: he knows
the most terrible things I've done, every stupidity,
inadequacy, awkwardness,
ignorance, the mad girl I screwed
because she once again and again
teased and rejected me, and whose psychic incompetence
I grimly greeted as an occasion for revenge;
he greets my voice

with an interest, and regard, and affection,
which seem to signal I'm worth love;

—you finally
forgave me for being your son, and in the nasty
shambles of your life, in which you had less and less
occasion for pride, you were proud
of me, the first Bidart
who ever got a B.A.; Harvard, despite
your distrust, was the crown;—but the way
you eyed me:
                    the *bewilderment*, unease:
the somehow always
tentative, suspended judgment . . .

—however *much* you tried (and, clearly,
you *did* try)
                    you could not remake your

taste, and like me: could not remake
yourself, to give me

the grace
needed to look in a mirror, as I often can
now, with some equanimity . . .

VIII

When did I begin to substitute
insight, for prayer? . . .

                            —You believed in neither:
but said, "My life is over,"
after you had married Shirley,
twenty-five years younger, with three
small children, the youngest
six months old; she was unfaithful
within two months, the marriage was simply
annulled . . .
                    A diabetic, you didn't
take your insulin when you drank, and
almost managed to die
many times . . .
                    You punished Ruth
when she went to Los Angeles for a weekend, by
beginning to drink; she would return home
either to find you in the hospital,
or in a coma on the floor . . .

                            The exacerbation
of this seeming *necessity*
for connection—;
                    you and mother taught me
there's little that's redemptive or useful
in natural affections . . .

I must *unlearn*; I must believe

you were merely a man—
with a character, and a past—;

        you wore them,
        unexamined,

like a nimbus of
furies

round your
greying, awesome head . . .

I X

What should I have done? In 1963,
you wanted to borrow ten thousand dollars
from me, so that we could buy cattle
together, under the name "Bidart and Son,"—
most of your money was tied up
in the increasingly noxious "Bidart Brothers,"
run by your brother, Johnny . . .

I said no,—
that I wanted to use the money
for graduate school; but I thought
if you went on a binge, and as had happened
before, simply threw it away . . .

The Bidarts agreed
you were *not* to be trusted; you accepted
my answer, with an air
of inevitability I was shocked at . . .

I didn't *want* to see your self-disgust;
—somehow, your self-congratulation
had eroded more deeply, much
more deeply, than even I had wished,—

but for *years*, how I had wished! . . .

I have a friend who says
that he has never felt a conflict
between something deeply wished or desired,
and what he thought was "moral" . . .

Father, such innocence
surely is a kind of *Eden*—; but,
somehow, I can't regret that we
are banished from that company—;
in the awareness, the
history of our contradictions and violence,
insofar as I am "moral" at all,
is the beginning of my moral being.

x

When I began this poem,
                    to see myself
as a piece of history, having a past
which shapes, and informs, and thus inevitably
limits—
          at first this seemed sufficient, the beginning of
freedom . . .
                    The way to approach freedom
was to acknowledge necessity:—
I sensed I had to become not merely
a speaker, the "eye," but a character . . .

And you had to become a character: with a past,
with a set of internal contradictions and necessities
which if I could *once* define, would at least
begin to release us from each other . . .

But, of course, no such knowledge is possible;—
as I touch your photographs, they stare back at me
with the dazzling, impenetrable, glitter of mere life . . .

You stand smiling, at the end of the twenties,
in a suit, and hat,
cane and spats, with a collie at your feet,
happy to be handsome, dashing, elegant:—

and though I cannot connect this image

with the end of your life, with the defensive
gnarled would-be cowboy,—

you seem happy at that fact, happy
to be surprising; unknowable; unpossessable . . .

You say it's what you always understood by freedom.

1968–69

Part Three

Vergil Aeneid *1. 1–33*

Arms and the man I sing, the man and hero, who
driven by fate, by the gods' mere force and Juno's hate,
found Italy, found Latium, the man and hero
battered on land and sea, who founded our city,
brought us gods and lineage,
even to this, garlanded walls of substantial Rome.
    Muse, make me mindful of the causes, load upon me
knowledge of her sorrows, she whom men call the queen of the
        gods
but driven to drive the most earnest of men
to such misfortunes. After foundering Troy,
what human being would not have been satisfied?
    An ancient city, held by farmers, fronting Italy
and the mouth of the Tiber, then
magnificent in elegance, rich in courage:
such was Carthage—it is said, the city of Juno, and loved
by her even above Samos, seat of her shrine.
She wanted this new home of her weapons and chariot
first among men. But the fates did not so spin:
bathed in the faded pageant of Troy, in rue and despair,
a race was to come to rule over men,
merciless in war, graceful in victory.
She had heard that beloved Carthaginian Libya
would soon be a level plain.
Within her mind the resistless past returned:
scenes of burning Troy, herself as chief of destruction—
and deeper, to the causes in insult and wounded love
and proper mother's pride, Paris's
judgment, the bastard

founding of the city, Ganymede snatched above her own
    daughter:
out of this the Trojans must wander, must wander in error
seeking over the world's seas
what the remnant left by the Greeks and merciless Achilles
may never enjoy through the will of the queen of the gods:
how heavy the burden, to found the Roman race.

AFTER CATULLUS

The day was calm . . . For the usual reason
I had gone into the country, and indeed
there seemed peace. Understanding friend:
with whom only
I can be frank; can even you
receive this as I received it?

I walked down into a field. The lions were in bloom,
crocus, hyacinth, coxcombs,
shouting to be so full of sun and seed.
I said to myself: "I must lie down."
They touched my face. I
could not see the sun.

In this darkness then: a sound became clear,
half-moaning
half-delight
of a girl—twelve?—lying
not five feet from me
with her legs spread apart. Above her in jeans

a boy maybe younger worked away . . . He was good!
But he didn't see me standing staring with blind eyes
in the sun. She resisted: his arms held her arms
firmly down
as the open front of his jeans disappeared
under her dress. I
put him to the sword!

With my prick.

TO MY FATHER

I walked into the room.
There were objects in the room. I thought I needed nothing
from them. They began to speak,
but the words were unintelligible, a painful cacophony . . .
Then I realized they were saying
                                    the name
of the man who had chosen them, owned them,
ordered, arranged them, their deceased cause,
the secret pattern that made these things order.
I strained to hear: but
the sound remained unintelligible . . .
senselessly getting louder, urgent, deafening.

Hands over my ears, at last I knew
                                    they would remain
inarticulate; your name was not in my language.

ANOTHER LIFE

Peut-être n'es-tu pas suffisamment mort.
C'est ici la limite de notre domaine. Devant
toi coule un fleuve.
VALÉRY.

"—In a dream I never *exactly* dreamed,
but that is, somehow, the quintessence
of what I *might* have dreamed,

            Kennedy is in Paris

again; it's '61; once again
some new national life seems possible,
though desperately, I try to remain unduped,
even cynical . . .

           He's standing in an open car,

brilliantly lit, bright orange
next to a grey de Gaulle, and they stand
not far from me, slowly moving up the Champs-Elysées . . .

Bareheaded in the rain, he gives a short
choppy wave, smiling like a sun god.

—I stand and
look, suddenly at peace; once again mindlessly
moved,

       as they bear up the fields of Elysium

the possibility of Atlantic peace,

reconciliation between all that power, energy,
optimism,—

        and an older wisdom, without
illusions, without force, the austere source
of nihilism, corrupted only by its dream of Glory . . .

47

But no—; as I
watch, the style is

    not quite right—;

    Kennedy is *too* orange . . .

And de Gaulle, white, dead
white, ghost white, not even grey . . .

       As my heart
began to grieve for my own awkwardness and
ignorance, which would never be
soothed by the informing energies
      of whatever
wisdom saves,—

    I saw a young man, almost
my twin, who had written
    'MONSTER'
in awkward lettering with a crayon across
the front of his sweat shirt.
      He was gnawing on his arm,

in rage and anger gouging up
pieces of flesh—; but as I moved to stop him, somehow
help him,
    suddenly he looked up,

and began, as I had, to look at Kennedy and de Gaulle:

and then abruptly, almost as if I were seeing him
through a camera lens, his figure

split in two,—
>   or doubled,—

and all the fury
>   drained from his stunned, exhausted face . . .

But only for a moment. Soon his eyes turned down
to the word on his chest. The two figures
again became one,

and with fresh energy he attacked the mutilated arm . . .

—Fascinated, I watched as this
pattern, this cycle,
>   repeated several times.

Then he reached out and touched me.

—Repelled,
>   I pulled back . . . But he became
frantic, demanding that I become
the body he split into:
>   'It's harder
to manage *each* time! Please,
give me your energy;—*help me!*'

>   —I said it was impossible,
there was *no part* of us the same:
we were just watching a parade together:
(and then, as he reached for my face)
>   leave me *alone!*

He smirked, and said
I was never alone.

I told him to go to hell.

He said that this was hell.

                        —I said it was impossible,
there was *no part* of us the same:
we were just watching a parade together:
                                when I saw

Grief, avenging Care, pale
Disease, Insanity, Age, and Fear,
                        —all the raging desolations

which I had come to learn were my patrimony;
the true progeny of my parents' marriage;
the gifts hidden within the mirror;

—standing guard at the gate of this place,
triumphant,
            striking poses
                        eloquent of the disasters they embodied . . .

—I took several steps to the right, and saw
Kennedy was paper-thin,
                        as was de Gaulle;
mere cardboard figures
whose possible real existence
lay buried beneath a million tumbling newspaper photographs . . .

—I turned, and turned, but now all that was left
was an enormous
            fresco;—on each side, the unreadable
                        fresco of my life . . ."